Wonder witch

Helen Muir

Illustrated by Linda Birch

Macdonald

For Ronan
and Lorcan Browne

Wonderwasp

This witch had all a witch could want. She had a tall hat, a black cat and a broomstick.

She could turn people into toads if she wanted to, but she was getting a bit tired of that old trick.

"Nothing funny ever happens to me," she said, stuffing six jelly babies into her mouth.

The witch loved sweets and she adored jewels. Best of all though she enjoyed jokes.

She split her sides when the black cat sat on a wasps' nest. That bad old thing laughed till she cried.

"What a smashing joke!" she kept saying. "I must get a sting myself. Being a witch is so boring. I think I'll turn into a wasp."

She tried out some spells:

> *"Bumpety plumpety plackety ping*
> *Give me... um... thin black legs and blackened wing*
> *Dazzling stripes and... er... a SUPER sting!"*

She felt a bit dizzy then she went all orange and her wings started to grow.

By morning she was a wasp.

She put her hat on and flew up to the mirror. She admired herself, dancing and flying, and tried out a loud angry buzz.

"... zzz... zzzzzzzZZ... ZZZZZZZ!"

"Yippee!" she shrieked. "Now for some fun! Here comes Wonderwasp...!"

For her first joke Wonderwasp flew off to find the cat who was, of course, sitting on the mat.

She dive-bombed his head, crawled along his back and buzzed loudly in his ear. "Zzzzz…zzzzzzz!"

Actually, she was laughing so much she could hardly buzz.

But the cat hated wasps. His fat paw flew out and smacked her hard on the nose. Wonderwasp spun dizzily to the ground.

She wasn't put off easily though. There was a dog next door.

"Dogs are more stupid than cats," she said thoughtfully, settling for a short rest on a red jelly baby. "I"ll give that dumb creature a few surprises."

She soared over the hedge and landed on the dog's bone. She waited, shaking with laughter.

"Zzz... zz..."

But the dog hated wasps. It nipped her, drenched her in slobber and buried her with the bone.

Shortly after, the dog dug up his bone (and the witch) and carried them into the house. He buried the bone behind a cushion and poor Wonderwasp crawled out along the sofa.

She was fast asleep when the dog's big fat master sat on her.

She stung him.

That man went mad. He hated wasps. He rolled up a newspaper and started shouting. The dog barked, tea was spilt and chairs overturned. It was a terrible rumpus!

Wonderwasp was knocked out against the window and left for dead on the sill.

Well, she wasn't dead but she wasn't laughing either. She could see that being somebody else was not as much fun as she'd thought.

Wasps had problems too. Being a wasp was no fun at all. She was absolutely exhausted.

She crawled slowly up the window.

Wearily she buzzed the magic words:

*"Yumpety bumpety tackety titch
For heaven's sake make me a WITCH!"*

She grew red in the face. Her wings dropped off and turned into dust. As the cackling voice grew louder, a black-stockinged leg started swinging from the window-sill.

The dog stirred uneasily and growled in his sleep.

His master had dozed off for a minute so he didn't see a thing either.

The sitting room window suddenly opened wide. There was a gust of cold air and the witch was gone.

After that the witch was always on about wasps and what a terrible time they had. She forgot about guzzling jelly babies or gloating over her jewels because she was too busy talking.

"Laugh if you will," she exclaimed, "nobody enjoys a joke more than I do but there's nothing funny about being a wasp."

When the cat found another wasps' nest, the witch hurried out to it at once.

"Welcome home, my poor old friends!" she cried. "Why does everybody hate you?"

"Zzzzzz... zzzz... zzzzzzz... zzz... z!"

She was stung on the nose.

The black cat laughed fit to bust.

Witch Wonderwasp looked extremely hurt then she laughed too. After all, she did love a joke.

Wonderdog

When it was growing dark each evening, the witch went out for a spin on her broomstick. She sailed high above the trees, flying her kite.

If there were any dogs playing in the park, she raced them. Only animals could see her when she was on her broomstick.

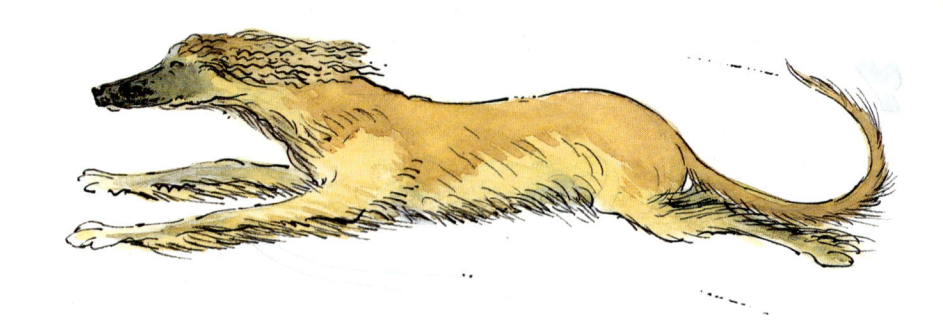

There was just one dog who could go faster than the witch. He was a big silky Afghan hound with a long nose. He danced along, tossing his head, until his owner let him off the lead. Then he went like the wind.

"Being a dog must be the best thing in the world," said the witch.

If there was a race, naturally the witch liked to win it.

She was cross when she didn't win.

"Bad dog!" she squawked, swooping round the dog's head to show him she meant business. "Sit!"

He jumped up and nipped a piece out of her black cloak. They both fell into the park pond.

A few days later, the witch saw a picture of that dog in a newspaper. He'd won first prize at the dog show. The champion's name was Lord Snouter of Perivale.

"Poof!" said the witch spilling tea all over her new track suit.

In the park, everybody admired Lord Snouter with his red rosette.

"He's going to the Afghan Races now," his owner said. The Afghan Races were held each month to raise money to look after lost or unwanted dogs.

The champion hurtled across the grass, in and out of the trees.

The witch raced too. Her hat fell over her eyes and she was knocked off her broomstick by a branch.

After that, the witch began some racing training herself. She hid her jelly babies, where she wouldn't find them, and went on a diet. She was determined to beat Snouter.

On the day of the races, masses of sleek, barking Afghans arrived at the racetrack. There were balloons, ice-creams and music. Lots of children came to watch.

The witch appeared in a sweat band and running vest. "We'll soon see who the champion is," she said, doing some press-ups.

While the dogs lined up, the witch hovered in the air on her broomstick.

The Starter dropped his flag.

They were OFF!

They went like the wind, Snouter leading. The witch rode straight into the balloons and nose-dived into a cowpat. She had to go and lie down in the first-aid tent.

Lord Snouter of Perivale had won the Wonderdog Silver Trophy. Everybody was patting him. He nipped the witch in the tummy as she limped past on her way home with a black eye.

"Shocking!" she said to a man in a wool hat, who was wandering about with a choke-chain as if he was looking for a dog.

"I want to win that Wonderdog Trophy," the witch said. "Being the champion Afghan hound must be absolutely smashing." She started muttering:

"Give me thickest fur and plate-like paws. Yellow fangs and... um... fiercest jaws!"

She turned into a monstrous dog with ears like aeroplane wings and a tail with spikes on it. People screamed. They wouldn't let her near the races.

Now the witch's plans became more cunning. The night before the next race, she hid behind a tree in the park. She had put down an ENORMOUS meal of bones, biscuits and meat.

She cackled as she watched the champ gobble the lot. Then the dog staggered home and fell fast asleep.

Next morning, a mystery Afghan lined up beside fat sleepy Snouter for the Wonderdog Trophy. The witch had turned into a beautiful creature with silky hair and a curly tail. Everybody was asking where she'd come from.

She curled her lip at the other dogs.

Then they were OFF!

They streaked away.

"Come on, Snouter!" yelled all the children.

But poor puffing Snouter was beaten. His tail was between his legs as the new Wonderdog pranced about.

"Our winner will be worth a fortune," the Judge said. "Where is the proud owner?"

The organisers were bewildered.
Nobody knew.

"I own that dog!" The choke-chain man in the wool hat pushed through the spectators. Before Wonderdog could escape, he snapped the chain round her neck. He led her forward to the children's cheers and took the Silver Trophy.

Alas, the man was no dog lover. He was a dog stealer. He threw the dog into his garage while he ate a hearty supper.

Being a champion had turned out to be the worst thing in the world. Wonderdog was hungry and tired, and whined sadly, wishing she was at home with the black cat.

"*Shurrup!*" shouted the dog stealer. "You don't need any supper. You'll be sold tomorrow."

But when the dog stealer went to the garage in the morning, Wonderdog had vanished! The witch was already at home, stuffing herself with jelly babies.

"Never again!" she told the black cat, shaking some long Afghan hairs off her hat. "You wouldn't believe the skulduggery in dog racing."

The witch still goes out each evening and Snouter and she race together.

Of course he never mentions the Wonderdog Trophy. Nor does she.

Now he's getting older, she can beat him easily. But she doesn't try.

Not often, anyway.

The dog stealer still looks for Wonderdog. But he keeps away from the park because he always falls in the water.

Falls?

Well, there's never anybody around. Only a batty old person in a black hat.

Wonderphone

Another thing the witch loved was telephoning. When she saw a telephone, she usually stopped to play a joke.

Sometimes she rang her friend, Witch Wotnot, but she also played tricks on a lot of people she didn't know.

She dialled 999 and called the fire brigade when Witch Wotnot didn't invite her to her Bonfire Night fireworks party.

Firemen hosed the bonfire, Witch Wotnot and all the guests. The witch watched from behind a tree. She nearly died of laughter.

She hadn't forgotten the dog stealer who locked her in the garage without any supper. She ordered a load of manure to be dumped in his front garden. The stink was terrible!

The witch rang the local paper with the story of a terrible new illness with spots as big as sugar lumps. Worse than chicken pox. Worse than measles.

She painted huge red spots all over her face. Even the black cat laughed. People jumped out of her way in the supermarket. Children were sent home from school to stop them catching the disease.

More than anything, the witch enjoyed crossed lines. She was so nosey.

She adored listening to other people's conversations.

She made rude noises.

"Rubbish!" she'd say in a loud voice, "Why don't you take a running jump at yourself!" She had to hold her nose to stop cackling.

"The most exciting thing in the world," the witch said to the black cat, "is to be a telephone." She shut herself up for some days while she thought out an exceptionally powerful spell.

There were bangs and flashes and weird warbles. Suddenly all the lights went out and the witch vanished.

Next morning there was a most peculiar-looking new telephone at the station.

Wonderphone gave out the time minutes late so passengers missed their trains. When the telephone weather forecast announced snow, the sun shone. If anybody dialled a pop song, the witch's singing was horrible.

If Wonderphone seemed a bit wonky, that was because the witch was so busy listening in to Witch Wotnot. Of course, Witch Wotnot was talking about *her.*

"She calls herself Wonderwitch," Witch Wotnot was saying, "but she's only a stupid old boot."

"I'll turn her into a toad's toenail," raged the witch. But now she was a telephone, she couldn't.

While the witch was planning a punishment for Witch Wotnot, a man dropped coins into Wonderphone.

Pip... pip... pip!

"'allo Sid."

"'allo Bill."

"We gotter do a really really big job, Sid. Nicking videos and that, is nuffin."

Wonderphone rocked. Burglars!

Next day Sid and Bill had another conversation.

Pip... pip... pip.

"'allo Bill. I seen a nice little place full of gold and jewels and suchlike. I'm keeping watch. Belongs to some loony."

Wonderphone crackled. Nobody liked gold and jewels more than the witch!

She guessed it must be Witch Wotnot's house. She had gold and jewels and she was an ol' loony all right! Well, she wasn't going to warn that ratbag. Serve her right if she was burgled!

Soon, the two burglars laid their final plans.

"Meet you at midnight round the back of that 'ouse," Bill said to Sid.

The witch opened her mouth to ask the address. Out popped the weather forecast. *"Sunshine in the afternoon will be followed by heavy rain during the night."*

"Blimey!" gasped Sid, running off.

The witch couldn't stop laughing at the thought of Wotnot losing all her jewels and Wonderphone went even more wonky. If anyone dialled the weather forecast, they got the time instead.

Bill rang Sid and got Hong Kong.

Then a caller spilled ice-cream all over Wonderphone. Another punched her to get his money back.

When she'd sung twenty pop songs out of tune, the witch's voice was only a hoarse squeak. A notice was pinned on her saying 'OUT OF ORDER!'

She decided that being a telephone was far worse than being a wasp or a dog. Bashed and sticky, her face was squashed, her head ached and her voice was a whisper. She struggled to think of a spell.

"Weather forecasts,
pop songs, rings
Who cares about the
beastly things
I only want to be a witch
Turn me back without
a hitch!"

Unfortunately there was a hitch. The witch turned back into herself but on the way home she couldn't stop ringing. People stopped and stared.

Tired as she was she was still laughing to herself at the thought of that ol' loony Witch Wotnot losing all her treasures.

But she stopped laughing as she stepped into her own house. All her gold and jewels had gone! The house was empty except for the black cat.

The witch danced with fury.

But later, when they'd had supper, the witch calmed down.

"Oh well," she sighed, putting her arms round the black cat, "thank goodness they didn't find the jelly babies." She stuffed nine into her mouth.

"I'd better not play any more jokes. After all, I have all a witch could want. Being a Wonderwitch is the best thing in the world."

At that moment she looked out of the kitchen window to see Witch Wotnot skipping along in her leopard-skin mini-skirt and tiara.

"Just one more joke..." Wonderwitch murmured, and she threw the washing-up water out of the window. Witch Wotnot was soaked.

Wonderwitch and the black cat laughed so much they had to go to bed for two days.

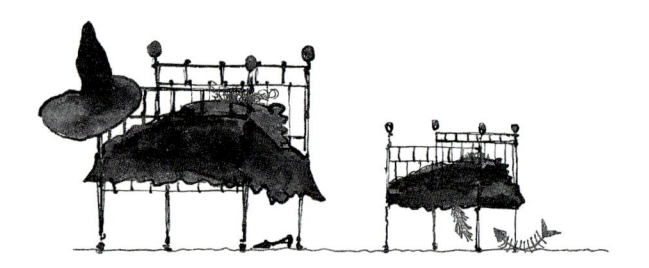